AZTEC DESIGNS

Wilson G. Turner

DOVER PUBLICATIONS, INC.
Garden City, New York

Dedicated to
my three sons
WILSON, CHARLES, *and* RUSSELL
With thanks to Beverley Trupe
for her assistance

Copyright

Copyright © 2005 by Dover Publications, Inc.
All rights reserved.

Bibliographical Note

Aztec Designs is a new work, first published by Dover Publications, Inc., in 2005.

DOVER *Pictorial Archive* SERIES

International Standard Book Number

ISBN-13: 978-0-486-44338-6
ISBN-10: 0-486-44338-8

Manufactured in the United States by LSC Communications
44338808   2020
www.doverpublications.com

INTRODUCTION

The Aztec had their beginnings in a band of wandering peoples who followed the word of their god Hummingbird Wizard, Huitzilopochtli (Wee-tsee-lo-*poch*-tlee), to the promised land of Tenochtitlán, which is now Mexico City, around the thirteenth century. In a short time, the Aztec conquered millions of peoples throughout Mesoamerica, exacting tribute in goods and slaves from all. Their culture ascended in the postclassic period of the other great Mesoamerican cultures—Maya, Toltec, Mixtec—after they had passed their zeniths.

Aztec art is difficult to separate from that of the Toltec or Mixtec or the Teotihuacán or other Mesoamerican peoples because in it, as well as in religion, political and military structure, and way of life, the Aztec incorporated much from those they conquered. In the process of assimilation, their tendency was to carry each adopted convention to the extreme. Another factor complicating identification of typically Aztec artifacts is diffusion. An object made in Tula, a Toltec city, might be found in the Aztec city of Tenochtitlán as the result of trade or tribute paid. On the other hand, an item manufactured in Tenochtitlán might be found in Puebla or Oaxaca.

This book is an attempt to present art forms that are exclusively Aztec, those that arose within the culture as it developed. Because the same subjects were depicted in all Mesoamerican cultures, the scholar must rely on his expertise and knowledge of the style of artwork to identify the origin of any particular piece. Scholars differ, however, on the culture to which a number of surviving artifacts belong. And in addition to the difficulty of distinguishing purely Aztec art forms from those of their contemporaries, there is that of the scarcity of objects that survived the European conquest. The early attempts to confiscate Aztec gold and the later attempts to destroy all objects associated with practices believed to be pagan were remarkably successful. Gold objects were sent to Europe, all but a few melted down for easier transport, and most of those arriving intact were subsequently melted down also. The temples, the statues, the books, the ornaments and implements were torn apart, smashed, burned. A few items survived as curiosities with minor damage, such as the breast plate (shown on page 6) sent by Cortez to the Spanish king. Archaeological excavation has revealed some buried artifacts that were not totally destroyed. Construction in Mexico City has also led to the discovery of long-buried objects, such as the stone disc depicting the moon goddess shown on page 2.

To modern eyes, as well as to the sixteenth-century eyes of the European conquerors, Aztec art may appear macabre or grotesque, due in part to its typical exaggeration of subjects the Aztecs considered sacred and natural but that may have opposite connotations in other cultures. For example, one of the primary Aztec deities was the serpent, often depicted as feathered. The human skull was represented both by itself and as an integral design element in other pieces of artwork. As mentioned before, the subjects, if not the manner in which they were depicted, were borrowed from earlier cultures and were represented throughout preconquest Mesoamerica.

Very few surviving Aztec artifacts are undamaged. In the drawings in this book, pieces have been restored to their original condition where that condition is known. The illustrations on pages 20, 21, and 38 are examples of restoration. In other examples, restoration was not possible because information is lacking (see, for example, page 36).

Some of the more famous Aztec artifacts, such as the calendar disc, have not been included here because they are extensively reproduced elsewhere.

WILSON G. TURNER

This stone sculpture is over eight feet tall. Coatlicue (Ko-ah-*tlee*-kway) is the mother of earth and the mother of gods. The circlets covering her skin represent turquoise and water, hence purity. The serpents of her skirt indicate mankind. The necklace of hands and hearts denotes sacrifice. The symbolism in this carving represents the life cycle—a continuous movement from life to death, death to life.

This huge carved stone disc (ten feet in diameter), was found accidentally by workers installing underground electric cables in Mexico City in 1978. It depicts the dismembered body of Coyolxauhqui (Coyol-*show*-kee), the moon goddess. Snakes decorate the headdress and bind each of the severed extremities and the waist. Scalloped edges depict severed flesh. Bones are shown protruding from arms and legs.

Known as the earth monster, the figure on this large basalt disc (43 inches in diameter) represents the sun in its nighttime aspect, when it was thought to pass beneath the earth toward the east to rise again at morning. It was believed that the monster devoured bodies of the dead as it passed. Both front and back of the figure are depicted in this Picasso-like arrangement of features. The inverted skull at center is a buckle on its back. The braids shown at top are the lower edge of the back of the skirt. Note the claws for hands and feet.

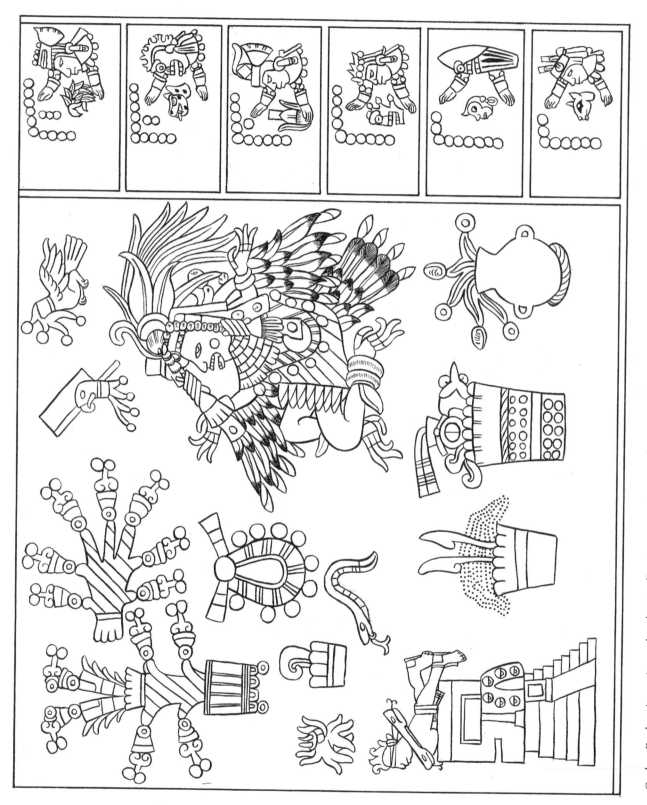

Codex Borbonicus. Aztec books (codices) were written with pictographic symbols. On this page the goddess Itzpapalotl (*Eets-pa-pa-lotl*) is shown surrounded by offerings and other items. The temple at bottom left with the human figure and spider above depict the realm of darkness. The two trees at top left represent the legendary homeland. The circles in the small framed drawings signify the names of the days. For example, on top right is 13 Eagle.

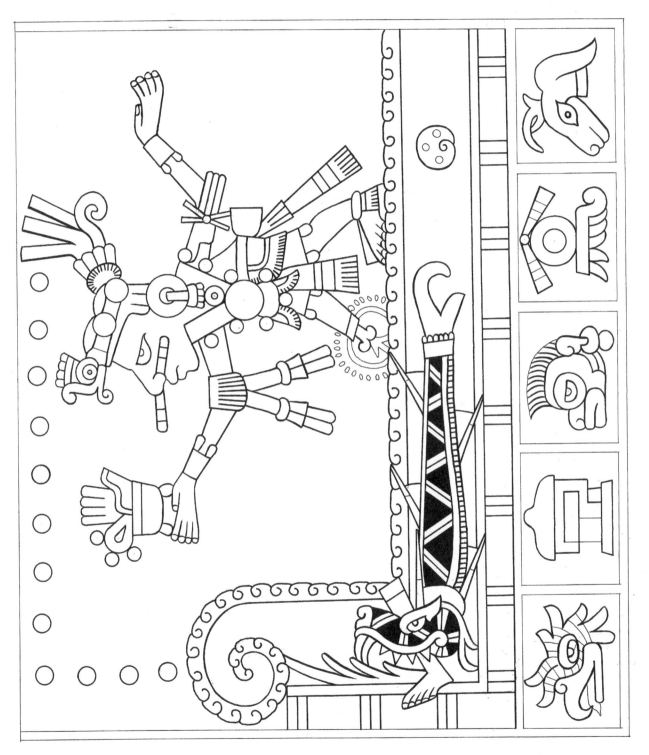

Codex Fejérváry-Mayer. Tezcatlipoca (Tehs-kah-tlee-po-kah), known as Smoking Mirror, one of the chief Aztec gods, tempted the earth monster with his foot as bait. Her jaw was ripped off in the struggle, preventing her from returning to the depths and thereby creating the earth from her body.

This double-headed serpent is from a mosaic breastplate that the Emperor Montezuma sent as a gift to Cortez. The pieces of the body are assorted shades of blue and green turquoise. The eye outline and nose are red. The white teeth and fangs and pink gums are made of shell.

Aztec slit drum. Made of basalt rock, this drum has a clear, bell-like tone. The carved face is of Macuilxochitl (Mah-kweel-*sho*-cheetl), Five Flower, a synonym for Xochipilli (see pages 16 and 18), god of music. The eyes are stylized hands and mouths. The cheek designs are human hearts. The carved motifs at the ends represent jaguar skins; that at the base, a woven mat.

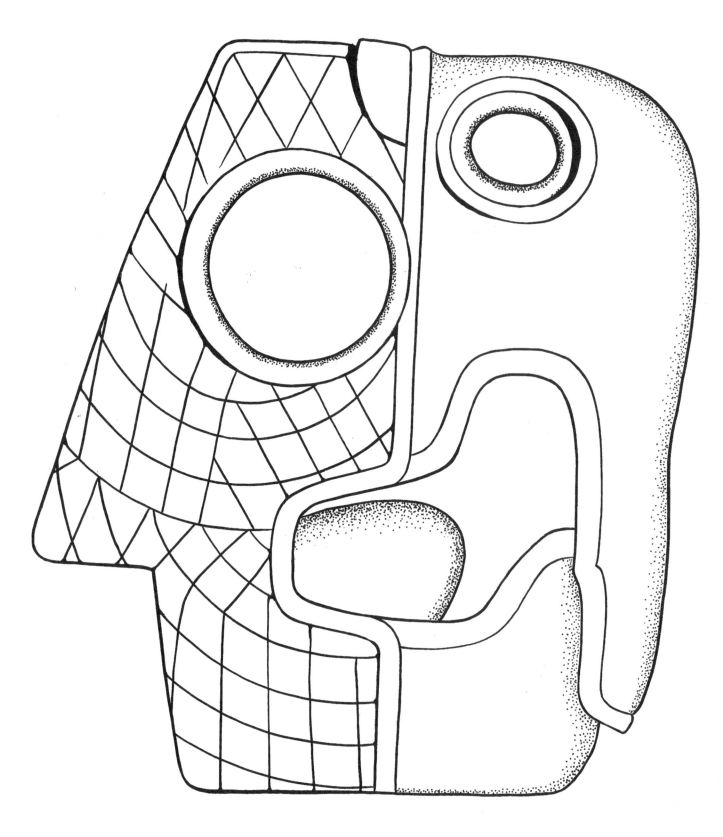

Ball-court marker. This carved basalt macaw head was used by the Aztecs as a court marker in one of many forms of the sacred ball game prevalent in all pre-Columbian Mesoamerican cultures. Sometimes the outcome of the game was prearranged, giving a theatrical feeling to the religious event.

The ashes of the Aztec ruler Ahuítzotl (Ah-*weet*-sotl), who preceded Montezuma II, were kept in this stone box. The carved lid shows the water beast surrounded with symbols for water (see page 13 for the side of the box).

This talking skull is carved on the side near the top of a model of a pyramid, a monolith of a temple of the sacred wars. Speech is indicated by the design emerging from its mouth. The design is a pictograph of water and fire, signifying a sacred war. The large circle at lower right represents the number "one." Together, the skull and number give the date of One Death.

This feather shield with the whirlpool motif is an aspect of the goddess Lady Precious Green, Chalchihuitlicue (Chal-chee-weetl-*ee*-kway). The large areas of the design are colored feathers. Black feathers form the outlines. This artifact is well preserved except for a scar on the upper middle of the face and some damage to two fangs (center and second from right). The drawing shows the piece as it would have looked originally.

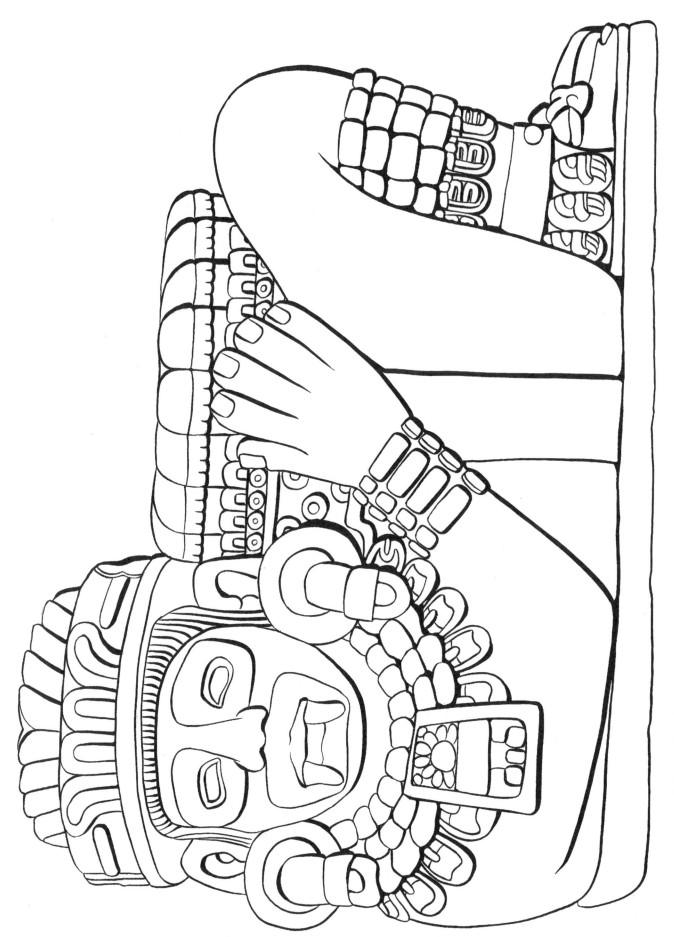

In this full round sculpture we see a Tlaloque (Tlah-*lo*-kee), one of the aides of the god Tlaloc (Tlah-lok), holding a bowl. Normally the aide would pour water from the bowl, but in all likelihood this one held the hearts of sacrificial victims.

Here a Tlaloque pours rain from his bowl. Notice the corn symbols also pouring out and the convoluted designs scattered around, representing clouds. The medallion hanging from his necklace is the symbol for the planet Venus. This detail is from the side of a stone box that held Ahuitzotl's ashes (see page 9).

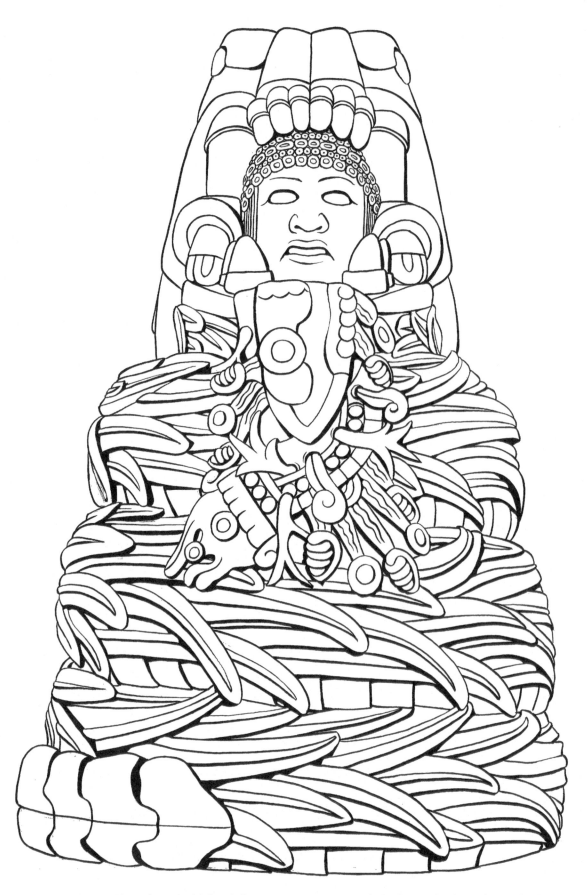

Quetzalcoatl (Ket-sahl-*ko*-ahtl), a primary Aztec god, is shown here as the god of the planet Venus from within the jaws of the earth god. Symbolism is prominent here, as in most Aztec sculpture. The serpent's tongue represents the knife of sacrifice. Drool from under the tongue is the symbol for water and a sacrificial heart. Notice the serpent's tail, which identifies it as a rattlesnake.

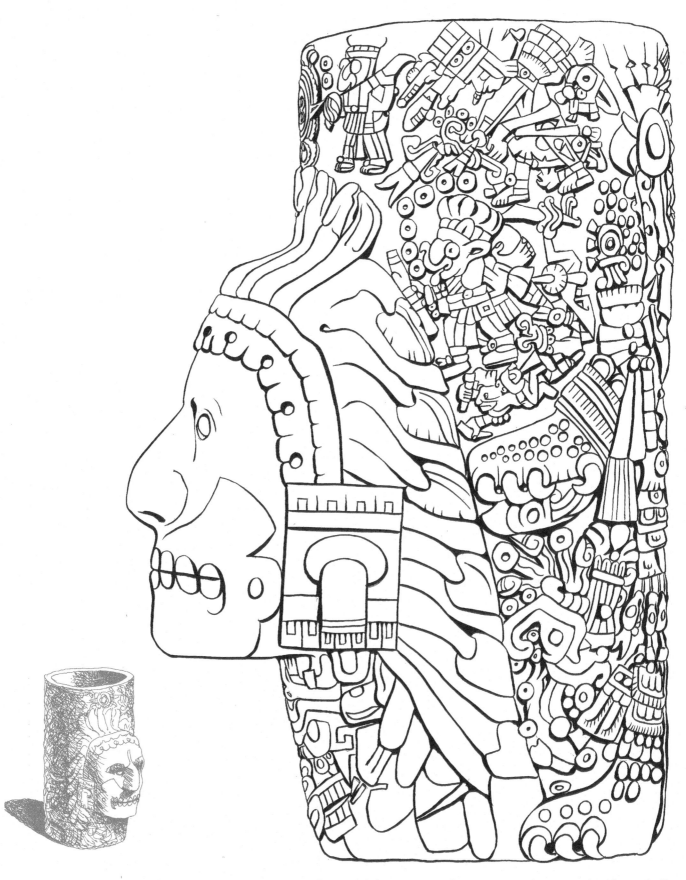

The Bimilek vase. This stone vessel, part of the treasure of Montezuma, is covered with symbolic Aztec designs. The mask over the mouth is part of the hieroglyph for movement, such as that of a heartbeat or earthquake (see the olin bowl on page 31). The water plants on the large headdress symbolize earth, as do the jaguar paws. Sacred water is indicated by the circles and shells under one of the paws. Among the small designs are jaguar gods and other gods, including Tlaloc, the god of rain. Note the resemblance to a North American Indian with headdress.15

A person costumed as Five Flower, Macuilxochitl, synonymous with Xochipilli (see pages 7 and 18), god of vegetation and music, is carried in a procession by two young warriors. Another warrior leads the procession blowing a conch shell. From the post-Columbian Codex Magliabecciano, now in Florence, Italy.

Terra-cotta braziers of this sort were used to burn copal, a sacred incense. The black smoke suggested rain clouds and was used in rites of sympathetic magic to induce rain. The figure is a Tlaloque.

The Flower Prince, Xochipilli (Soh-chee-*pee*-lee), is the Aztec god of music, dance, and worldly pleasures (see pages 7 and 16). This is one of the most sensitively carved sculptures extant from the Aztec era. There were once rattles in its hands to accompany the singing. The broken nose of the carving is shown restored in the drawing.

18

Earth and Venus. Here the feathered serpent represents earth and the human features represent Venus (see page 14). This stone sculpture of porphyry is unique in design and workmanship. Notice that the human head emerges from the mouth of the serpent, but the four human limbs are outside and wrapped around the feathered body. In full-round sculpture, the artist usually removes all stone unnecessary to the finished piece and along with it any trace of the stone's original shape. The artist carved this figure to fit the original shape of the stone without loss of realism in the subject. In the example on page 14, no hint of the original shape of the stone remains in the finished carving. Conversely, in the carving shown on page 12, sacrifices were made in subject matter to maintain the rectilinear shape of the original material. Neither method is better than the other: the choice was a matter of the personal preference of the sculptor.

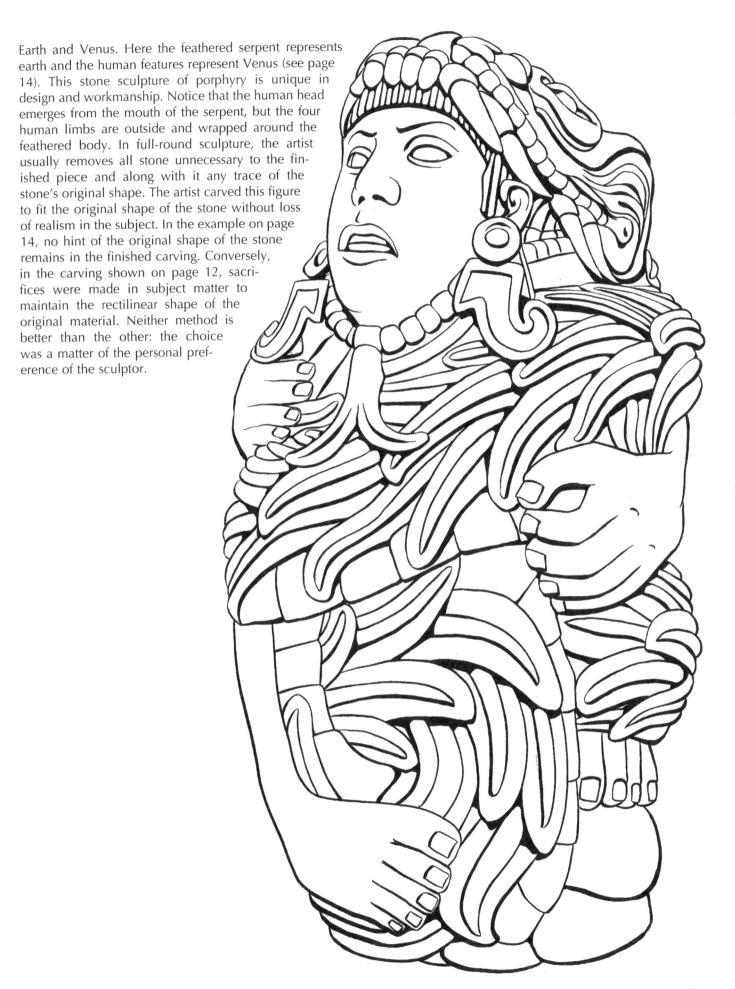

Page 65 of the *Codex Borgia.* Quetzalcoatl as the wind god Ehecatl (Ay-*hay*-kahtl) faces another figure, perhaps a slave, across water. A female figure kneels beside the water. The circlets within circles behind the god and on his clothing represent water. The dark circles under his legs and feet indicate jaguar skin (royalty). The codex

page from which this drawing was made is damaged, as are many Aztec artifacts. In this drawing, the bottom row of pictographs has been restored. On page 53 of the *Codex Vaticanus B* virtually the same allegory is drawn in a completely different style but with many of the same symbols.

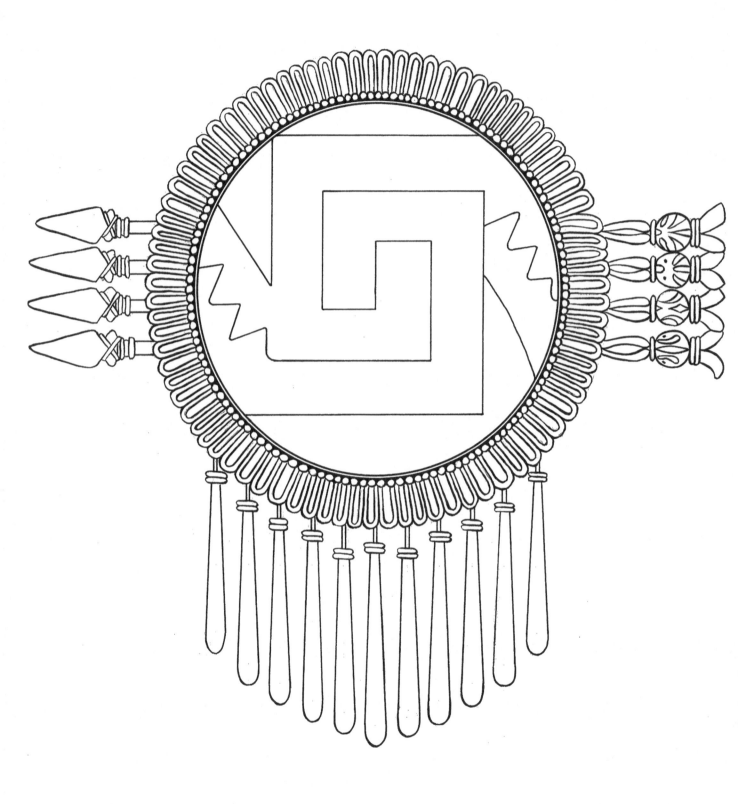

The design on this war shield was used to depict war on many
items, such as breast plates and medallions. This shield was made
of gold inlaid with turquoise and other semiprecious stones.

Feathered Shield. On this decorative shield, the coyote—one version of the Aztec god of fire—is shown as a feather mosaic. The outlines of the design are made of narrow strips of gold. Teeth and claws are cut from thin sheets of gold.

The goddess Coatlicue (Ko-ah-*tlee*-kway) in the guise of a young woman. As with all Aztec deities, Coatlicue has many aspects. In this example she is both young and poised to attack the dead.

This representation of the Aztec goddess of agriculture, Xochiquetzal (Soh-chee-*keh*-tsal), Flower Bird, is a 21-inch basalt sculpture. Her belt is a rattlesnake. Damage to the top of the headdress has been repaired in this drawing.

A detail from the *Codex Borgia* calendar. Here, in the guise
of the planet Venus, Quetzalcoatl is shown on the days he
is a threat to the god of mountains, Tepeyollotl (Teh-peh-*ol*-
lotl), and all things represented by that deity.

Gods of death and wind. Symbolism permeated Aztec life and works. These two figures, from the *Codex Borgia,* display some of the many symbolic meanings of the circle. The death eye, represented by a circle bisected with a line, appears not only on the god of death but on the headdress and costume of the wind god. The circlet within a circle means water. There are many of these on the figure of the wind god. Circles enclosing loops and lines are cockle shells meaning earth. Groups of circlets on the death god's body imply pustules of sickness and death. Circles at top and bottom of the page represent count marks or numbers. The platform beneath the figures depicts a skull inverted, opened out, and flattened.

This jadeite figure was of great beauty to the ancient Aztec, although it may appear grotesque today. It is a version of Xolotl (*Sho-lotl*), twin brother of Quetzalcoatl, representing the planet Venus as the evening star.

This back view of the carving on the previous page depicts the sun, which must die each night as the evening star rises.

The earth god Tlaltecuhtli (Tlahl-teh-*koo*-tlee) is depicted in this outside view of the bowl shown on page 31. The Aztecs believed the earth god must be supplied with sacrificial human hearts to prevent earthquakes and destruction of the present world. The skulls represent sacrificed victims.

Olin Bowl. The design in the center of this bowl, called olin in the Nahuatl language of the Aztec, means movement, as in heartbeat or earthquake. Carved from jadeite, it received the still-beating hearts of sacrificial victims.

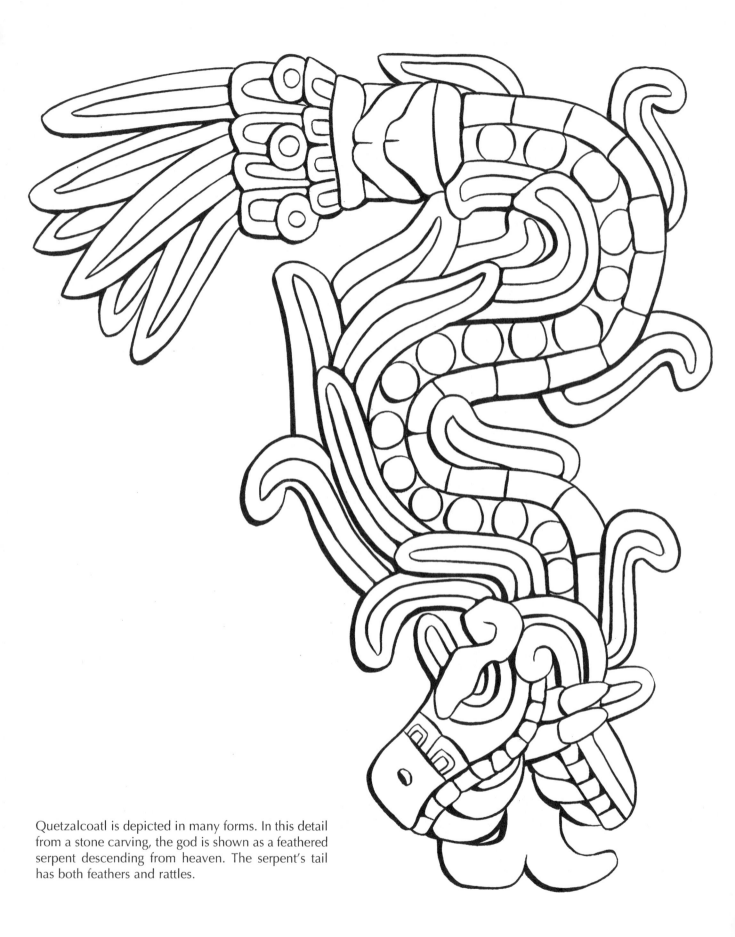

Quetzalcoatl is depicted in many forms. In this detail from a stone carving, the god is shown as a feathered serpent descending from heaven. The serpent's tail has both feathers and rattles.

Stone of Tizoc. The emperor Tizoc (*Tee*-sok), in the guise of Huitzilopochtli, the blue hummingbird god. Note that one of his feet is a feather. Tizoc is shown here in one of 15 encounters carved on a stone 8 feet in diameter and 2 feet thick. His holding the other figures forelock connotes his capture of a city. The name of the city in each encounter is represented by a design above the captive's left shoulder.

4   3

The Aztec wrote from right to left. The above sequence prophesies the potential condition of the life-sustaining corn (maize) crop for four succeeding years. (1) In the first panel, at far right of the next page, Chalchihuitlicue, the water goddess, is shown with storm clouds extending from her headdress and forming a hand that pours an overabundance of water on the corn plants. Notice the saturated ground. (2) The next panel shows the year overseen by the lord of jewels, signifying that it will be a very dry year. Notice the digging stick broken from working the hard ground. Overhead are clear nights (the tear shapes are stars) and fluffy clouds without a sprinkle of rain.

The goddess of fertility, Mayahuel (Mah-yah-*hoo*-el), had 400 sons. She was also goddess of the maguey plant, from which the native liquor, pulque, is made. Mayahuel is shown here with a turtle and a serpent, sitting in front of one maguey plant and holding another in a pot. From the *Codex Laud.*

2   1

(3) The third year is depicted under the auspices of Tlaloc, the god of life-giving water. Here the perfect soil condition is shown. The corn is plump and healthy and the digging stick unbroken. (4) Xipe Totec (*Shee*-peh *To*-tehk), the flayed one, controls the fourth year. The prospect is bleak. The ground is hard and dry. Birds and burrowing animals devour seeds before they sprout. A noisy crow hovers above. Notice that the corn god has been unable to get roots into the ground as shown in the previous panels.

Tlazolteotl (Tlah-sol-*teh*-ahtl) is another Aztec fertility goddess. In this aspect she resembles our stereotype of a witch. She wears a pointed hat, sits astride a broom with an animal familiar, which in this case is a red snake, the Aztec symbol for sex. From the *Codex Fejérváry-Mayer*.

A fragment of one of four sides of an Aztec square stone altar. Carved in relief, it depicts four warriors in full regalia. This piece is badly damaged.

A fresco at Tizatlan. The god Tezcatlipoca, known as Smoking Mirror, was the antithesis of the god Quetzalcoatl. One of the primary Aztec gods, Tezcatlipoca was the god of night and sacrifice.

Lady Precious Green. The goddess in this sculpture controls all sudden storms and whirlpools (see page 11). Tlaloc, the rain god, is her husband. The missing top of the head of this piece has been restored in the drawing.

A stone tablet representing the moon. The Aztec saw a rabbit in the dark areas of the full moon where European folklore tells of the man in the moon. Next time the moon is full, step outside and see what you think.

This depiction of the feathered serpent was the foot of a stone balustrade on one of the most important temple pyramids at Tenochtitlan (Mexico City). It is one of the few remaining artifacts from this site, which was sacked and razed by Cortez's army in the sixteenth century.

40

The feathered serpent was a prominent diety in Mesoamerica even before Quetzalcoatl and Kukulcan (Koo-kool-*kahn*). It has been found in panels similar to this in nearly all archaeological sites of the various cultures, from Aztec to Mixtec, from Toltec to Maya.

This terra-cotta eagle symbolized the sun. Here it is eating a human heart, symbolic of the sun replenishing itself. (It is possible that this is a Toltec piece rather than an Aztec one. But it is made exactly as the Aztec depict their warrior cult, the Eagles.)

INDEX